The Best 50
BAR DRINKS

Dona Z. Meilach

BRISTOL PUBLISHING ENTERPRISES
SAN LEANDRO, CALIFORNIA

Printed in the United States of America.

ISBN: 1-55867-257-5

Cover design:	Frank J. Paredes
Cover photography:	John Benson
Illustration:	Hannah Suhr

BAR DRINKS

There are literally thousands of bar drinks. A few books list as many as 2500 recipes. A commercial bartender may know two hundred drink recipes, but generally his clients request between 40 and 50 different drinks. These include mixed drinks, cocktails, shooters and variations. In this book, you'll find a quick reference for the top favorites.

VARIETIES

A **mixed drink** is one that combines an alcoholic beverage with a mixer and is served over ice in a 6- to 12-ounce glass. Examples are Scotch and soda, gin and tonic, vodka and orange juice (a Screwdriver), vodka and tomato juice (a Bloody Mary), or rum and coke.

A **cocktail** is what most people think of as a "drink." This includes highballs and martinis. Mixing a cocktail is more involved and can

range from the simple 2-ingredient gin-and-vermouth classic dry martini, to a Pink Lady, Grasshopper, or very fancy concoction with blends of rum and fruit garnishes. A cocktail is usually stirred, shaken or blended, as opposed to simply poured like a gin and tonic. It is usually served in a stemmed glass.

A **shooter** is a class of drinks served in a shot glass, (1 to 2 oz.) and meant to be swallowed in a single gulp. Their formulas are similar to mixed drinks but they are more potent because the ratio of alcohol to mixer is higher. Today, some are modified for sipping. Shooters aren't even listed as such in older bar mixing books.

Variation: A **slammer** is of a shot of tequila or other spirit, with 7-Up or ginger ale added in a tall shot glass or an old-fashioned glass. The glass is then slammed on a hard surface (usually with a napkin beneath the glass), and a hand or another napkin placed on top of the glass so it doesn't fizz over the top. The drink is immediately chugged down while it is still fizzing.

A **hot drink** is some alcohol generally mixed with coffee, tea, or hot chocolate. Good for cold winter nights.

A **nonalcoholic drink** will keep you socially acceptable, prevent you from getting high, and will help you avoid arrest and fines if you're a designated driver.

WHAT'S GOOD? WHAT'S TRENDY?

Drink styles, preferences, and their names, have changed considerably over the years. Some drinks in books dating from the '60s and '70s aren't listed today, and vice-versa. Bartenders, like good chefs, often change classic recipes, and that calls for a name change. Yet classic drinks retain their names.

Drink preferences differ by geographical locations, and by weather. A Mint Julep has long been associated with the southern states. A rum drink on a hot summer day can have a different taste

reaction than one served in cooler weather. Some drinks taste better at different times of the day. There are drinks associated with a "cocktail hour" or "after dinner," and "bedtime." Drinks such as a Screwdriver or Fun on the Beach made with fruit juices are suggested for lunch or brunch. Champagne or light brandies are also morning drinks. A tall drink such as a Tom Collins or a gin and tonic are good afternoon drinks for people who linger over a drink and often spend more time twirling the ice in their glass than actually tippling.

Taller drinks to slake one's thirst and to replenish lost body fluids are considered "summer drinks." Winter drinks might have heavier ingredients, such as eggnog, and there are hot drinks such hot toddies, hot-spiced punch and hot cider concoctions. Brandy, whisky and rum are base liquors that mix well in hot drinks and help warm one's insides.

THE INGREDIENTS

Bar drinks require some alcohol content plus one or more other ingredients, called mixers.

Alcohol

The alcohol that is commonly the basis of drinks can be gin, vodka, whiskey, rum, bourbon, Scotch, tequila or flavored liquors.

Less common, but often-used liquors include flavored brandies and cordials or liqueurs, such as cherry brandy, apricot brandy, Triple Sec, amaretto, Cointreau, Kahlua, Irish Cream, Grand Marnier, champagne, wine and beer.

Mixers

A mixer might be: soda, tonic water, Coca-Cola, 7-Up, ginger ale, orange juice, pineapple juice, grapefruit juice, tomato juice, cranberry juice and heavy cream. Fizzy drinks should be used before they go flat. For fruit juice, cocktails use fresh juice.

Additional Ingredients

Other ingredients for the well-stocked bar are: sugar (either powdered or superfine) or sugar syrup (called simple syrup), grenadine, fine salt, bitters, Tabasco Sauce and Worcestershire sauce. Do not use granulated sugar such as you use on morning cereal as it won't dissolve. Flavored sugar can be purchased from a liquor store or a coffee shop.

Make your own simple syrup:

In a small saucepan over a high flame, combine 1 cup cold water and 3 cups sugar. Bring to a boil for a few minutes until sugar is dissolved. Remove from heat and allow to cool. Bottle it tightly; it will keep almost indefinitely.

Garnishes

Garnishes are used to flavor and decorate a drink. They can be olives, pearl onions, maraschino cherries, celery sticks, lemon, lime or orange peel twists, citrus fruit, kiwi or pineapple slices or wedges.

To prepare a lemon or orange twist: Remove the fruit ends, peel the skin from the top, remove it from around the fruit, and cut into 1-inch lengths, or cut $\frac{1}{4}$-inch lengths from the top to the bottom. Remove the white "pith" (it can leave a bitter flavor). Rub the outside of the peel around the rim of the glass to release the flavorful oils, twist the peel and drop it into the glass.

Nonfood garnishes are functional and decorative, or purely decorative. They may include fancy stirrers, swizzle sticks, straws, flags, umbrellas and plastic mermaids that perch on the side of the glass.

MEASUREMENTS TO KNOW

1 large jigger=	2 ounces	1 fifth=	⅕ gallon or 25.6 ounces
1 jigger=	1½ ounces	1 quart=	32 ounces
1 pony=	1 ounce	1 liter=	33.8 ounces
1 table-spoon=	3 teaspoons	750 milli-liters=	25.4 ounces
1 cup=	8 ounces	splash	a quick squirt
2 cups=	1 pint		

THE CHILLING FACTS ABOUT ICE

Ice is not just a cold cube of frozen water. The use of ice is an integral, often ritual, part of serving bar drinks properly. Almost all cocktails should be served in a prechilled or frosted glass. Here are some ways to accomplish this:

· Put glasses in the refrigerator for 30 minutes and, just before use, put them in a freezer for about fifteen minutes.

- For a frosty finish, dip the glass in water and then put it in the freezer.
- Before pouring a cocktail, fill the glass with cracked ice, stir or swish the ice around in the glass about six times, discard the ice, and then pour the drink into the glass.
- For a large party, fill a tub with cracked ice, keep the glasses in the ice, and use them as needed.
- Always use freshly made ice cubes from clean ice trays.
- For crushed or broken ice, use an electric ice crusher or a blender, or wrap cubes in a towel and hit with a mallet.
- The larger the piece of ice, the more slowly it will melt. Crushed ice melts fastest, shaved or cracked ice next, cubes melt slowest.
- Always put the ice in a glass first, and then add the liquid.
- Refrigerate vodka, gin, and other base liquors. They won't freeze because of the alcohol content. Refrigerate mixers such as soda, tonic and ginger ale.

BASIC TOOLS OF THE TRADE

Having professional bar tools makes mixing drinks more fun than using improvised kitchen tools. Once bought, these items will last forever. Generally, select stainless steel, glass, or plastic over aluminum. Aluminum can give a metallic taste to some drinks.

- Shot glass
- Measuring jigger
- Shaker (stainless steel or glass). Some shakers have the strainer built in at the top.
- Strainer
- Bar spoon
- Ice bucket
- Tongs
- Blender
- Bottle opener
- Corkscrew
- Pitcher
- Pourers
- Paring knife
- Muddler
- Cutting board
- Juice squeezer
- Swizzle sticks
- Straws
- Wiping cloths
- Coasters

INTRODUCTION

TYPES OF GLASSWARE

A drink will be more attractive and appetizing if served in a glass that enhances it. Some drinks originally served in an old-fashioned glass may be served "up," meaning in a stemmed glass. Often, drinks normally served up may be served in an old-fashioned glass "on the rocks," meaning over ice cubes. The function of a stemmed glass is to provide a place to hold the glass so your hands won't dilute or warm the cold liquid.

- Stemmed cocktail glass 4 oz.
- Old-fashioned or rocks glass 6 oz.
- Highball and Collins glasses 8 oz. to 12 oz.
- Wine glass
- Cordial glass
- Champagne glass (flat saucer-shaped and flute-shaped)
- Margarita glass
- Martini glass
- Snifter
- Whiskey shot glass
- Whiskey sour glass
- Beer stein
- Coffee mug

BARTENDING TECHNIQUES:
MIXING — WHETHER 'TIS BETTER
TO SHAKE, STIR OR BLEND

That is the question that even bartenders ponder. Many bartenders dramatize their drink-mixing methods and develop a style or flair for which they become known. One may shake a drink a given number of times, or a certain distance from his body, or overhead or over chest height. For stirred drinks, they may have a prescribed number of times they stir, in a particular kind of container. They may even insist that a customer return a drink that varies from being mixed according to their prescribed routine.

Shaking a Drink

Drinks consisting of heavy-density ingredients are usually shaken in a cocktail shaker. These are cream drinks, juices, egg drinks and syrupy liquors. Shaking produces a cloudier-looking drink, and creates a fizz or foam, which is preferred for some drinks.

First put the ice in the bottom part of the shaker, and then add the other ingredients. Insert the top part of the shaker into the bottom part. Grab the shaker in both hands so that one hand is on each end. Raise the shaker to shoulder level and shake vigorously forward and backward over your shoulder until the shaker feels cold, about ten times. (Too long a shake will dilute the drink). Separate the two halves, lay a strainer across the top of the mixing glass, hold it in place with your index finger, and strain the drink into the serving glass. Some shakers have holes in the top half for straining.

Stirring a Drink

Drinks with ingredients that are light or clear and will blend easily are stirred. These include vermouth, gin, tequila, tonic, ginger ale or soda. Stirring results in a clearer-looking drink than one that is shaken. The object is to stir the ice silently and mix it gently without "bruising" the gin or other liquor.

Pour the ice in a glass or cocktail pitcher and add the ingredients. With the back of the bar spoon touching the side of the glass, rotate the spoon around the glass and twirl it in your finger so the back of the spoon stays against the glass. Stir only ten or twelve complete rotations so you don't dilute the drink. Remove the bar spoon, put the strainer in place and pour the liquid into a chilled glass.

Blending a Drink

Blending involves mixing the drink in an electric blender as opposed to a hand shaker. A pina colada and a margarita are mixed in a blender, giving the drinks froth on top.

Muddling

A muddle is a wooden or metal stick with a bulb-like ending that is used to crush ingredients in the bottom of a glass. These might be a cube of sugar, a berry, a mint leaf or a piece of fruit added to

give flavor or color. Tamping the ingredient with the round end of the muddler a few times usually produces the desired result.

Frosting the Rim of a Glass with Salt or Sugar

There are two ways to frost the rim of a glass with salt or sugar. If the drink uses a fruit garnish such as a lemon, lime or orange wedge, use the wedge to moisten the glass's rim before adding ice or liquid. Run the wedge around the rim and while still wet, dip the rim into a shallow saucer of fine salt or sugar. If no garnish is used, place the glass rim upside down on a clean wet sponge, and then dip the rim into the fine salt or sugar. Granulated sugar is best because it crystallizes and remains hard on the rim.

Note: All recipes in this book are for a single serving unless otherwise noted.

'57 CHEVY

This drink may bring back memories of old cars, drive-in movies and singing while driving. This is strictly a nostalgia drink, but it's quite potent, so don't drink while you drive.

1 1/2 oz. Southern Comfort
1/2 oz. vodka
1/2 oz. Grand Marnier
pineapple juice
1/2 oz. grenadine, optional

Pour all ingredients over ice in a shaker, strain into a highball glass and fill the glass with pineapple juice. Orange juice or other fruit juices may be substituted or combined.

Southern Comfort
vodka
Grand Marnier

ALABAMA SLAMMER

Southern Comfort already contains bourbon and brandy, along with peaches and herbs, so this combination of spirits could make any southern gentleman forget his manners. This is not a "slammer" that is slammed on the bar; it's the name of the drink.

1 oz. Southern Comfort
$\frac{1}{2}$ oz. sloe gin
1 oz. amaretto
1 dash lemon juice

Pour Southern Comfort, gin and amaretto over ice in a highball glass and stir. Add a dash of lemon juice and serve.

Southern Comfort
sloe gin
amaretto

B-52

When these liqueurs are poured carefully into a glass, they will layer on top of one another for a colorful drink. Each layer can be sipped separately for its flavor, or the drink can be stirred. Serve in a cordial glass or — more elegant — in a stemmed wine glass.

1/3 oz. Kahlua
1/3 oz. Irish cream liqueur
1/3 oz. Grand Marnier

Build in the order given by pouring into the glass over the back side of a bar spoon. The result will be three layers. Do not use ice. Other liqueurs, such as amaretto and Triple Sec, may be substituted for Grand Marnier. Always begin with the heaviest liqueur and graduate to the lightest on the top for the layered, built effect.

Kahlua
Irish cream liqueur
Grand Marnier

BAHAMA MAMA

Drink one of these, close your eyes, and you'll think you're on a vacation in the Bahamas listening to the palm trees sway in the balmy breeze.

¹/₂ oz. gold rum
¹/₂ oz. coconut rum
¹/₂ oz. banana liqueur
¹/₂ oz. grenadine
1 oz. orange juice

Put this all in a blender or shaker with ice. Blend or shake and strain into a highball glass.

rum
banana liqueur

BLOODY MARY

Harry's New York Bar, Paris was the birthplace for this popular drink and the actress Mary Pickford was the inspiration for spicing it up from the original vodka and tomato juice mixture. Different bartenders have added Worcestershire sauce, the celery stick garnish, and other ingredients through the years.

4 oz. tomato juice
1 oz. lemon juice
2 oz. vodka
½ tsp. prepared horseradish
1 dash Worcestershire sauce
1-2 dashes Tabasco Sauce
pinch celery salt
black pepper
celery stalk and lime wedge for garnish

Pour tomato and lemon juices over ice in a highball glass. Add vodka, horseradish, Worcestershire sauce, Tabasco Sauce, celery salt and pepper and stir. Or shake: put ingredients in a shaker, shake sharply, and strain into a glass. Garnish with a wedge of lemon over edge of glass, and a celery stick. Serve with a stirrer.

EASY VARIATION
1 1/4 oz. vodka
4 oz. commercially prepared Bloody Mary mix

vodka

BLUE LAGOON

Something old, something new, here's a drink that's both — and it's blue. Harry's son originated it at Harry's Bar New York, in Paris. He made it with lime juice originally, but today it's more popular with lemonade. Try it both ways. The traditional garnish is a maraschino cherry and a slice of lemon or lime. Use a red or blue maraschino.

1 oz. vodka
1 oz. blue curaçao
lime juice or lemonade
maraschino cherry and slice of lemon or lime for garnish

Pour ingredients over ice in a highball glass.

*vodka
curaçao*

BRANDY ALEXANDER

Here's a classic drink with a dessert-like taste, but with a definite kick. It has a rich, dark color and an iced coffee heritage.

1 oz. dark crème de cacao
1 oz. cream or ice cream
1 oz. brandy or cognac
grated nutmeg for garnish

Put ice in a shaker. Pour in crème de cacao, add cream, and then add brandy. Shake sharply and strain into a stemmed cocktail glass. Garnish with grated nutmeg.

crème de cacao
brandy

COSMOPOLITAN

A lovely pink color and refreshing flavor make this an ideal ladies' drink and a decorative adjunct for luncheon and bridal shower tables. Add a garnish appropriate for the occasion. Try a pink ribbon around the base of a stemmed glass.

1 1/2 oz. vodka
1 oz. Cointreau or Triple Sec
1 oz. lime or lemon juice
3 oz. cranberry juice
lemon or lime twist for garnish

Fill a shaker with ice, vodka, Cointreau or Triple Sec, lime or lemon juice and cranberry juice. Shake until well chilled and strain into a martini glass. Garnish with a twist of lemon or lime.

vodka
Cointreau or Triple Sec

CLASSIC DAIQUIRI

The daiquiri, a true classic cocktail, was brought to America from Cuba. It was enormously popular during the presidency of JFK, whose favored drink it was.

1 ounce Bacardi Light rum
1/2 ounce lime or lemon juice
3/4 tsp. sugar or simple syrup

Mix rum, lime, and sugar in a shaker with ice. Strain into a chilled cocktail glass or serve on the rocks.

rum

DAIQUIRIS WITH FRUIT

VARIATION #1 — STRAWBERRY DAIQUIRI

With frozen strawberries available year-round, the strawberry daiquiri has become a popular drink. Freeze the berries in season by spreading them in a single layer on a baking sheet uncovered. When frozen, pack them in a plastic bag for storage and use when needed. Or buy them already frozen without the syrup.

3 cups sliced strawberries, or
1 pkg. (12 oz.) unsweetened frozen strawberries (do not thaw)
2-3 tbs. light rum
2-3 tbs. sugar
1 tbs. lime juice

Put all ingredients in a blender container and process until smooth. If the machine struggles to process frozen strawberries, let stand at room temperature for about 10 minutes to thaw slightly, and then process. Pour processed mix into a margarita or other stemmed cocktail glass. Serve immediately, or store in the freezer. About 5 to 15 minutes before serving, place the drink in the refrigerator or on the counter to soften sufficiently for serving.

OTHER VARIATIONS
Banana
Pineapple
Orange

Makes 4 drinks.
rum

FUN AT THE BEACH #1

Fun on the Beach drinks also masquerade under the names, "Sex on the Beach," or "A Day at the Beach," depending upon the person serving them. They can be made with different juice combinations such as peach, pineapple and orange juice. Midori has a melon flavor and Chambord is a dark purple liquid made with small black raspberries and other fruits and herbs with honey.

1 ½ oz. vodka
¾ oz. Midori melon liqueur
½ oz. Chambord
1 ½ oz. pineapple juice
1 ½ oz. cranberry juice

Combine all ingredients in a shaker with cracked ice. Shake and strain into a chilled highball glass with ice cubes.

vodka
Midori and Chambord

FUN AT THE BEACH #2

When it comes to favorites, it will depend on the combinations of fruits that you like. Amaretto is made from apricots and almonds. Here it is combined with peach schnapps that gives it an entirely different, but still fruity, flavor.

1 oz. vodka
1 oz. peach schnapps
1 oz. amaretto
$\frac{1}{2}$ fill orange juice
$\frac{1}{2}$ fill cranberry juice

Shake and strain into a chilled highball glass with ice cubes.

vodka
peach schnapps
amaretto

FUN AT THE BEACH #3

Any of several versions of this popular drink earn rave reviews. "Safe Sex on the Beach," perhaps. When the liquor and liquors are omitted and the juices are mixed with a touch of grenadine, it is called "Safe Fun on the Beach" and is a nonalcoholic drink.

1 oz. vodka
3/4 oz. peach schnapps
1/2 fill cranberry juice
1/2 fill grapefruit juice
1/4 oz. Chambord, optional

Mix everything with cracked ice in a shaker and mix. Pour into a chilled highball glass.

*vodka
peach schnapps*

FUZZY NAVEL

National Distillers, which is now Jim Beam, introduced this popular drink. Someone thought up the name because it seemed clever and marketable — and they were right. The touch of peach flavoring gives it a smooth fruity taste.

1 1/4 oz. peach schnapps
3 oz. freshly squeezed orange juice

Pour schnapps over ice into a rocks glass and fill with orange juice. Stir well. A spritz of soda may be added.

peach schnapps

GILLIGAN'S ISLAND

This delicious fruity drink is scrumptious when served over ice. It's a pretty drink, thanks to the cranberry juice color, and nice for meetings and festive meals. It's not too alcoholic because it's mixed with fruit juices.

1 oz. vodka
1 oz. peach schnapps
3 oz. orange juice
3 oz. cranberry juice

Combine ingredients over ice in a shaker. Shake; do not stir. Pour over an ice cube.

*vodka
peach schnapps*

GIMLET

Rose's Lime Juice is a sweetened lime-flavored drink. Although used as a sweetened substitute for fresh lime juice, it really has a unique flavor of its own. Opinion is divided as to which makes the true gimlet: gin or vodka. You can experiment and substitute other spirits also.

$2\frac{1}{4}$ ounces gin or vodka
$\frac{3}{4}$ ounces Rose's lime juice

Stir with cracked ice; strain into chilled cocktail glass.

vodka or gin

GRASSHOPPER

This wonderfully frothy, refreshing mint green drink is meant to be sipped slowly. It's a perfect ladies' drink for a romantic predinner date. One is just right — drink two and you might begin hopping.

1 1/2 oz. green crème de menthe
1/2 oz. white crème de cacao
1 oz. light cream

Mix together with cracked ice in a shaker. Or put into a blender and blend until smooth. Strain into a margarita glass. Serve with a cocktail straw.

crème de menthe
crème de cacao

HARVEY WALLBANGER

The story is that the drink originated when a young surfer named Harvey lost in a surfing championship, and later drowned his sorrows in vodka and Galliano at Pancho's Bar in Manhattan Beach, California. To ease his frustrations, he banged his head against a wall until his friends stopped him.

3/4 oz. vodka
5 oz. orange juice
1/2 oz. Galliano
orange, lemon or lime garnish
maraschino cherry, optional

Pour vodka and orange juice over ice in a highball glass. Stir, and slowly pour Galliano into the glass over the back of a bar spoon. Garnish with a slice of orange, lemon or lime on edge of glass and add a maraschino cherry if you like. Serve with a stirrer and a straw.

vodka
Galliano

HOT TODDIE

Sip this drink on a cold winter's night sitting around a lit fire at home or at a ski resort. Some people prescribe it as the preferred remedy for fighting a cold.

1 tsp. sugar
boiling water
1 1/4 oz. brandy, bourbon, schnapps or choice of liquor
fruit for garnish

In a mug, add 1 tsp. sugar and your choice of liquor. Fill with hot water. Garnish with a citrus twist, apple slice or other fruit.

brandy or whiskey

HURRICANE

It is told that this drink was created at Pat O'Brien's bar in New Orleans in 1933. Its reputation has spread so that now it has been bottled ready to serve. If you can't get to New Orleans you can simulate the drink with this recipe.

1³⁄₄ oz. dark rum
4 oz. pineapple juice
2 oz. orange juice
splash grenadine
orange, strawberry for garnish

Combine ingredients over ice in a shaker and shake sharply. Strain into a collins glass, or a tall highball glass. Garnish with an orange wheel pierced with a strawberry on a toothpick. Serve with a straw and stirrer.

rum

IRISH COFFEE

Nothing beats sipping Irish coffee on a cold winter's night. But it is popular all year around, especially at the Buena Vista Bar in San Francisco. That's where the first Irish whiskey was served in 1952 after it was "imported" from a bar in Ireland.

3 sugar cubes
1³/₄ oz. Irish whiskey
3¹/₂ oz. hot coffee
²/₃ oz. heavy whipped cream

Pour whiskey into an 8-ounce glass mug that has been preheated with hot water. Add sugar and stir to dissolve. Add hot coffee and stir with a silver spoon. Gently pour lightly whipped cream over the back of the spoon so it floats on top of the coffee. Do not stir.

Irish whiskey

JELL-O SHOT

This variation on a shooter, originally welcomed by the college crowd, is now a popular mainstream item. Jell-O Shooters are meant to be sucked rather than sipped or downed. Use 2 oz. paper soufflé cups from your party store, or the paper cups your dentist uses. The iced concoction can be pushed up as it melts — the most convenient way to eat it.

1 small package Jell-O, any flavor.
1 cup boiling water
1 cup vodka or whiskey or
other favorite liquor or liqueur

Prepare a small package of berry or lime Jell-O according to the package directions. After mixing with 1 cup boiling water, let cool for about 15 minutes. Then substitute vodka or other liquor for the cold water called for in the instructions.

Pour into small 1½-ounce or 2-ounce paper soufflé cups (available at party shops). Use less liquor if you want the resulting cubes to be very firm. Store cubes in the refrigerator on a flat tray and they're ready to serve.

vodka or whiskey

VARIATIONS
lime Jell-O and tequila (Jell-O Margarita)
orange Jell-O and vodka (Jell-O Screwdriver)
strawberry Jell-O and rum (Jell-O Daiquiri)
pineapple Jell-O and coconut rum (Jell-O Pina Colada)
lime Jell-O, Triple Sec and vodka (Jell-O Kamikaze)

JOLLY RANCHER

Here are two recipes with slightly different flavors and colors. Either may be served as a shooter or in a highball glass over ice.

Shooter Recipe	**Highball Recipe**
1/4 oz. Midori melon liqueur	2 oz. vodka
1/4 oz. peach schnapps	1 oz. Midori melon liqueur
1/4 oz. rye whiskey	cranberry juice
3/4 oz. vodka	

Shake with ice and strain into a shot glass, or for the high-ball version, shake and serve over ice in an old-fashioned or highball glass.

> Midori
> vodka
> peach schnapps
> whiskey

KAMIKAZE #1

The Kamikaze was first meant to be a shooter, downed in one gulp. But now there is a modified version. Use the shooter recipe for gulping and the highball recipe for sipping.

Shooter Recipe	**Highball Recipe**
¹/₂ oz. vodka	1 ¹/₂ oz. vodka
¹/₂ oz. Triple Sec	1 oz. Triple Sec
¹/₂ oz. lime juice	2 oz. lime juice
lime wedge for garnish	lime wedge for garnish

For the shooter, mix with cracked ice in a shaker. Strain into a shot glass and garnish with a wedge of lime. Or, strain into a chilled highball or old-fashioned glass. Add a wedge of lime for garnish, and serve with a stirrer.

vodka
Triple Sec

KAMIKAZE #2

Here's another version of the Kamikaze with added ingredients for the stout of heart.

1 oz. gin
1 oz. vodka
1 oz. white rum
1 oz. tequila
1 oz. Triple Sec

1 oz. lemon juice
1 oz. orange juice
1 wedge lemon
1 splash cola

Pour all ingredients over crushed ice in a shaker. Shake, and strain into a highball glass.

gin
vodka
rum
tequila
Triple Sec

LIQUID COCAINE

This drink is aptly named; the combination is like taking a "high" orally.

1/4 oz. vodka
1/4 oz. Grand Marnier
1/4 oz. Southern Comfort
1/4 oz. amaretto
1 splash pineapple juice

Put cracked ice in a shaker, add vodka with liquors, and add a splash of pineapple juice. Shake well and strain into a shot glass.

*vodka
Grand Marnier
Southern Comfort
amaretto*

LONG ISLAND ICED TEA

There are about 10 variations of this drink, but this one wins a "popularity" award. Its strange name comes from the Oak Beach Inn in the Hamptons, on Long Island and originated with the bartender, Robert "Rosebud" Butt.

<table>
<tr><td>1/2 oz. vodka</td><td>juice of 1/2 lemon</td></tr>
<tr><td>1/2 oz. tequila</td><td>1 splash cola</td></tr>
<tr><td>1/2 oz. light rum</td><td>lemon or lime twist for garnish</td></tr>
<tr><td>1/2 oz. gin</td><td></td></tr>
</table>

Add ice to a chilled highball glass; pour in vodka, tequila, rum and gin. Add a dash of cola for coloring. Garnish with a lemon or lime twist.

vodka
tequila
rum
gin

MAI TAI

Mai tai are the Tahitian words for "the best," and the drink is so named because two Tahitian customers first tasted it and expressed their appreciation with the words, "Mai tai."

1/2 oz. rum
3/4 oz. curaçao
1 oz. lime mix
1 oz. pineapple juice
1/2 oz. grenadine

1/2 oz. simple syrup mix
1 dash orgeat (almond) syrup
fruit piece and mint leaf for
garnish

Pour all ingredients over ice into a shaker or blender and mix. Strain and pour over ice into a Collins glass. Garnish with a mint leaf, cherry, pineapple wedge or any combination of fruit available. Serve with a straw and stirrer.

rum
curaçao

MANHATTAN

When a drink has the name of a city, you can bet a local bartender originated it. History attributes this drink to New York City's Manhattan Club in 1874, when Winston Churchill's mother was entertaining a politician and lawyer, Samuel J. Tilden. Much later, there was a Hollywood movie titled "Manhattan Cocktail."

³/₄ oz. sweet vermouth
2¹/₂ oz. blended bourbon
dash Angostura bitters, optional

1 maraschino cherry
orange twist

Combine vermouth, whiskey, bitters, and ice in a stemmed, chilled cocktail glass. Stir gently to avoid bruising the spirits and clouding the drink. Place cherry in glass and strain whiskey mixture over cherry. Rub orange peel over glass rim and twist it over the drink to release oils, but don't drop it in.

sweet vermouth
bourbon

BASIC MARGARITA

The margarita was invented in 1948 when Margarita Sames, in Acapulco, Mexico, mixed her two favorite spirits, Cointreau and tequila. Her loving husband had her name etched onto a glass and thus was born the margarita.

1 oz. tequila
1 oz. Cointreau or Triple Sec
2 oz. sweet and sour mix or margarita mix, or lime juice
lime wheel for garnish

Rub lime on the rim of a margarita glass and dip rim in a dish of fine salt. Put ingredients into a blender with crushed ice. Blend until slushy and pour into prepared glass. Garnish with a lime wheel placed over the edge of the glass.

tequila

FROZEN MARGARITAS — QUICK AND EASY

Here's a quick and easy frozen margarita recipe. For other flavors use different and appropriate frozen juice concentrates such as lemonade, fruit, etc.

1 can (12 oz.) frozen Minute Maid limeade concentrate
¾ can tequila
½ can Triple Sec or Cointreau
1 lime, cut into circular slices
salt, optional

In a blender, add a full can of frozen limeade. Use the empty limeade can for measuring; add ¾ can tequila and ½ can Triple Sec or Cointreau. Add more tequila for a stronger drink. Fill blender with ice and blend. Add more ice while blending until blender is full.

tequila

MIDORI MARGARITA

Midori, a melon-flavored green liqueur, results in a beautifully colored, delicious margarita. It can be served in a highball glass instead of a margarita glass.

1 1/2 oz. tequila
1 oz. Midori melon liqueur
2 oz. sweet and sour mix
salt and lemon or lime juice for glass rim
lime wheel for garnish

Rub lime on the rim of a margarita glass and dip rim in a dish of fine salt. Put ingredients into a blender with about 1 cup crushed ice. Blend until slushy and pour into glass. Blend ingredients with crushed ice. Garnish with a lime wheel placed over the edge of the glass.

tequila
Midori

PEACH MARGARITA

Peach, banana, and strawberry margaritas top the flavor favorites. For a festive look, dip the rim of the glass in colored fine sugar instead of salt.

1 lime wedge
2 oz. peach slices with syrup
1¼ oz. gold tequila
½ oz. peach schnapps

½ oz. Triple Sec
1 oz. margarita mix
1 scoop crushed ice
peach slice

Rub the rim of a margarita glass with a wedge of lime and dip the rim into a saucer of sugar. Place all remaining ingredients into a shaker or blender. Mix and strain into the glass. Garnish with the wedge of lime and a peach slice.

*tequila
peach schnapps
Triple Sec*

CLASSIC MARTINI

Some believe that the martini was created in 1862 by a San Francisco bartender for a customer who wanted a cool drink before traveling to Martinez, a town 40 miles away, thus "martini." Others believe it was developed in New York much later by a bartender named Martini. In 1964, Sean Connery as British agent James Bond (007), popularized the vodka martini, that should be "shaken, not stirred" in the movie Goldfinger.

6-8 parts gin or vodka
1 part dry vermouth
crushed ice

Shake or stir gin and vermouth with ice. The ratio of gin to vermouth can vary according to taste. For a vodka martini, substitute vodka for the gin.

gin or vodka
vermouth

SAPPHIRE MARTINI

This makes a beautiful blue drink. Sapphire gin can be substituted for blue curaçao, and orange curaçao can be substituted for the blue curaçao.

2 oz. gin or vodka
1/2 oz. blue curaçao
lemon twist for garnish

Shake or stir gin and curaçao in a glass with crushed ice; strain into a martini glass. Garnish with a twist of lemon.

gin or vodka
curaçao

MATADOR

This is another nice, mildly sweet cocktail made with the very popular tequila as a base.

1½ oz. Tequila
3 oz. pineapple juice
1 oz. lime juice
½ tsp. simple syrup or to taste

Mix Tequila, pineapple juice, lime juice and syrup with cracked ice in a shaker. Strain into a chilled cocktail glass.

MIMOSA

This soft orange-colored bubbly drink was first served at the famed Pat O'Brien's bar in 1933, in New Orleans. It's so popular it's bottled as a ready mix. But if you can't get to New Orleans, the recipe here will simulate it.

3 oz. champagne, iced
5 oz. orange juice, cold
orange slice for garnish

Combine champagne and orange juice in a champagne flute or champagne glass and stir. Add an orange wheel on edge of glass. A nice touch is to pierce the orange with a flower on a toothpick.

champagne

MUDSLIDE

This is a rich, creamy dessert drink served in a tall hurricane glass. It tastes like a coffee milk shake but it can pack a kick — so sip it, don't guzzle it. This drink, originated by TGI Friday's, has become so popular that you can buy it premixed in single servings and large bottles, ready to pour over ice and serve. This recipe can be made with or without spirits and with or without the Hershey's Syrup.

$1/_2$ oz. coffee liqueur
$3/_4$ oz. Irish cream liqueur
$3/_4$ oz. vodka or rum
2 scoops vanilla ice cream
1 scoop crushed ice
1 tsp. Hershey's syrup

Place all liquid ingredients in a blender container, add crushed ice and blend lightly. Put Hershey's Syrup in a tall glass and swirl the glass so the syrup forms a swirl design on the inside of the glass. Quickly add blended liquid. It will freeze and hold the chocolate swirl against the glass.

coffee liqueur
Irish cream liqueur
vodka or rum

OATMEAL COOKIE

Some people save this recipe for the holiday season, but it is good all year around. It is a drink and NOT a cookie.

3/4 oz. Irish Cream liqueur
3/4 oz. amaretto
1/2 oz. cinnamon schnapps
1/2 oz. half-and-half

Put all ingredients in a shaker or blender with ice and mix. Strain and pour into a chilled rocks glass. This drink can also be served in a shot glass.

*Irish cream liqueur
amaretto
cinnamon schnapps*

OLD-FASHIONED

You don't have to be old-fashioned to drink this. It's still as popular as it was after the Civil War when it was created in honor of a retiring general. There are as many recipes for Old-fashioneds as there are bartenders. This one might become your favorite.

1 dash bitters
1 sugar cube
1 tsp. water
2 oz. rye whiskey or bourbon

lemon twist
orange slice and maraschino
cherry for garnish

Muddle bitters, sugar and water in an old-fashioned glass. Add whiskey and stir. Add ice and stir again. Rub lemon twist around glass rim. Garnish with an orange slice and a maraschino cherry. Note: Some bartenders recommend muddling the cherry and/or orange along with the bitters, sugar and water.

bourbon

PINA COLADA — CLASSIC, AND VARIATIONS

There are several ways to change a pina colada with flavorings other than pineapple. There is also commercially prepared pina colada mix. Serve a pina colada "up" (in a stemmed cocktail glass) or on the rocks. When the rum is replaced with vodka, it is called a "Chi Chi."

VARIATION #1 Classic Rum Colada
1 oz. light rum
2 oz. cream of coconut
2 oz. pineapple juice (or 2 oz. juice and 2 oz. crushed pineapple)

VARIATION#2 Peach Colada
2 oz. peach slices with syrup
1 1/4 oz. rum
3 oz. pina colada mix
1 scoop crushed ice

VARIATION #3 Strawberry Colada
2 oz. frozen strawberries
1 1/4 oz. rum
3 oz. pina colada mix
1 scoop crushed ice.
maraschino cherry and pineapple wedge for garnish (for all)

Blend rum, fruit, and juice for a few minutes, add ice and blend until smooth. Pour into a stemmed cocktail glass or serve on the rocks. Garnish with a maraschino cherry and add a pineapple wedge on a cocktail pick.

rum

POINSETTIA

Its name gives this drink away; serve it over the Christmas holidays when guests will especially enjoy the different taste, color and texture of this special drink.

$\frac{1}{2}$ oz. Cointreau
2 oz. cranberry juice
4 oz. cold champagne

Pour Cointreau and cranberry juice into a champagne flute and fill with champagne.

Cointreau
champagne

RUSTY NAIL

Unlike the Screwdriver, this drink didn't get its name because someone used a rusty nail for stirring. Rather it is named for the color that results from mixing Scotch and Drambuie. It certainly tastes better than it sounds. Serve this before brunch or lunch along with a choice of a Screwdriver or a Bloody Mary.

2 oz. Scotch
1 oz. Drambuie

Pour the Scotch and Drambuie over ice cubes into an old-fashioned glass. Serve with a stirrer and add a short straw for sipping if you like.

Scotch
Drambuie

SANGRIA

This is a favorite drink from Spain and is often made in large quantities to serve as punch. It is beautiful in a large bowl with fruit and floating ice blocks with flowers frozen within. Serve it in a punch bowl for a summer patio party.

4 oz. red wine (Cabernet Sauvignon or Burgundy)
1 oz. brandy
$\frac{1}{2}$ oz. cherry juice
$\frac{1}{2}$ oz. orange juice
fill glass with lemon-lime soda
assorted fruit: orange pieces, cherries, apple slices

Fill a tall glass with about $\frac{1}{2}$ cup ice. Add wines, brandy and juices, and stir. Fill glass with soda. Garnish with sliced or small chunks of oranges, cherries (if available) and apple.

wine
brandy

SCREWDRIVER

This is one of those drinks with a questionable origin. It is said to have originated in the 1950s when an American oilman, working in Iran, asked for orange juice in his vodka and stirred it with a screwdriver.

1 3/4 oz. vodka
5 oz. orange juice
orange slice and maraschino for optional garnish

Pour vodka over ice cubes in a rocks or highball glass. Add orange and stir. Garnish with an orange slice and maraschino cherry, and serve with a stirrer. Some people like to sip these through a cocktail straw.

vodka

SHIRLEY TEMPLE

This light rose-colored drink became popular in the 1960s when it was named for the popular child movie star. It is often referred to as a "mocktail." Grenadine, made from pomegranates, is red and sweet. This same cocktail is called a "Roy Rogers" when served to a boy!

³/₄ glass ginger ale, soda or sparkling water
¹/₂ oz. grenadine

Fill a tall glass about ¹/₃ with ice. Pour in ginger ale, soda, or sparkling water and add grenadine and stir. Garnish with a cherry and serve with a straw.

nonalcoholic

SIDE CAR

This is the early version of the now popular drink renamed, "Between the Sheets." The difference is that Between the Sheets has the addition of ¹/₂ oz. Benedictine that gives it a slightly medicinal, more piquant flavor.

¹/₂ oz. Cointreau
¹/₂ tsp. lemon juice
1 oz. brandy
orange peel for garnish

Combine all ingredients in a shaker with 3 to 4 ice cubes and shake vigorously. Strain into a chilled old-fashioned glass. Garnish with an orange peel. This may also be served "up" in a stemmed cocktail glass. Sugar the rim by rubbing with a cut piece of lime and dipping in a saucer of fine sugar.

Cointreau
brandy

SWEET TART

This drink's name is a cute play on words; the drink has both sweet and tart ingredients. Rose's Lime Juice is a special mixture with sugar added.

1 oz. vodka
1/4 oz. Chambord
1/4 oz. Rose's Lime Juice
1/4 oz. pineapple juice

Put all ingredients into a shaker with crushed ice and shake. Strain into a shot glass.

vodka
Chambord

TEQUILA MARIA

This variation of a Bloody Mary, made with tequila instead of vodka, is giving the original recipe competition as the popularity of tequila grows. You can buy commercially prepared Bloody Mary mix or make your own: use the recipe on pages 20–21 and omit the vodka.

1 1/4 oz. tequila
4 oz. Bloody Mary mix
lemon or lime slice or wedge for garnish

Mix tequila and Bloody Mary mix together. Pour over ice in a stemmed cocktail glass. Garnish with a slice or wedge of lemon or lime.

tequila

TEQUILA SLAMMER

Slammers have become popular recently. Use a sturdy shot glass or old-fashioned glass and soften the slam with a folded napkin beneath the glass so the glass doesn't break.

1 oz. tequila
3-5 oz. 7-Up or ginger ale

Pour tequila over a little ice in a tall shot glass or an old-fashioned glass. Fill glass with 7-Up or ginger ale. Place a napkin on the bar or other hard surface and place another napkin or your hand over glass. Slam glass bottom on napkin and the drink will fizz. Drink it down quickly while it is fizzy.

tequila

TEQUILA SUNRISE

This surprisingly colorful, tall drink, concocted in Mexico in the 1930s, is more popular than ever as tequila has become the "in" drink.

1 1/2 oz. tequila
3 oz. orange juice
3/4 oz. grenadine
lime wheel and maraschino cherry for garnish

Fill a clear, iced highball glass or tall wine glass with tequila and orange juice. Add grenadine slowly. Do not stir. As grenadine slowly drops to the bottom of the mixture, it fans out like the sun's rays. Garnish with a slice of lime over edge of glass and add a maraschino cherry. Serve with a straw and stirrer.

tequila

TOM COLLINS

Today's Tom Collins was originally called a John Collins, first mixed in a London coffee house around 1790-1817 using a Dutch-style gin. It only became popular when a London bartender used Old Tom Gin (a sweeter gin than the original, and made in London) and its name was changed to Tom Collins. Now, it's standard to make a Collins with London gin though other sprits can be used, such as brandy, rum, or whiskey.

2 oz. London gin
1 oz. lemon juice
1 tsp. superfine sugar
3 oz. club soda, Collins mix or Sprite
1 maraschino cherry
1 orange slice

In a shaker half-filled with ice cubes, combine gin, lemon juice and sugar. Shake well. Strain into a Collins glass almost filled with ice cubes. Add club soda. Stir. Garnish with an orange slice and a maraschino cherry.

gin

WHISKEY SOUR

This favorite drink of the 1950's has remained popular because of its slightly sour flavor. Originally it was made with brandy — a brandy sour — but whiskey is usually the preferred base today. Instead of lemon juice and sugar, the whisky may be mixed with 3 oz. prepared Sweet and Sour mix.

$1^3/_4$ oz. bourbon
$^2/_3$ oz. Rose's sweetened lemon juice
1 tsp. superfine sugar

Shake whiskey, lemon juice, and sugar (or prepared Sweet and Sour mix) with ice in a shaker, or mix for a few seconds in a blender with ice until foamy. Serve in a whisky sour glass or in a Collins glass over ice.

bourbon

VARIATION: AMARETTO SOUR

If you prefer the almond flavor of amaretto to whiskey, try this for a milder option to a whiskey sour. This drink will be sweet enough without sugar, unlike other sour recipes.

2-3 oz. amaretto
3 oz. sweet and sour mix (or ¾ oz. lemon juice)
orange slice

Put ingredient over ice in shaker and mix until foamy. Pour into a whiskey sour glass or over the rocks into an old-fashioned glass. Garnish with an orange slice.

amaretto

WHITE RUSSIAN/BLACK RUSSIAN

The use of vodka with white cream floating on top gives this sweet coffee-flavored drink its name. For a Black Russian, omit the cream; just mix together the vodka and Kahlua.

1 1/2 oz. vodka
3/4 oz. Kahlua or any coffee-flavored liqueur
1 oz. half-and-half or light cream

Put all ingredients in a shaker with ice and shake gently. Strain and pour over 2 ice cubes into an old-fashioned glass. Or omit the cream, follow the directions and make a Black Russian.

VARIATION
Lightly whip cream. Pour vodka and Kahlua over ice in the glass, and gently float cream on top. Serve with a stirrer.

vodka
Kahlua'

INDEX